Manifesting

Discover The Method To Unleash Your Boundless
Capacity, Materialize Your Ideal Life, And Attain All
Desired Goals Through The Utilization Of The Law Of
Attraction's Influence

Sebastian Ashcroft

TABLE OF CONTENT

The Influence Of Your Thoughts 1

The Foundational Principles Of Energy Medicine 13

How To Approach The Throne Of Grace For Answers 22

How Visualization Works 30

Humility Serves As The Yardstick For Measuring Spiritual Achievement 38

The Magic Of Manifesting 54

The Enigma Behind The Principle Of Attraction 63

Give It Your Best 72

Manifestation Of Happiness 75

Step 3- Convey Appreciation To The Universe 95

Being Optimistic 101

Below Are Several Advantages Of Practicing Fasting 125

The Influence Of Your Thoughts

Do you frequently ponder the reasons behind the success of individuals who may possess a lesser degree of intelligence or diligence in comparison to yourself? Have you ever contemplated the phenomenon of certain individuals effortlessly drawing wealth, love, and all the exquisite experiences life has to offer? The reason behind their knowledge surpassing yours is rooted in information that you are currently unaware of. They possess the ability to harness the power of their intellect in order to attract the multitude of positive experiences life has to offer.

Your mind is powerful. It boasts significantly higher capabilities compared to the most awe-inspiring human creation: the computer. On average, a typical computer has the capacity to store in excess of ten thousand songs and twenty thousand pictures. It is capable of storing a vast collection of high definition movies, reaching several hundred in quantity. Amazing, right? However, that pales in comparison to the formidable strength wielded by your intellect.

Your mental faculties are capable of executing ten quadrillion operations per second, and you remain unaware of this remarkable capability. That's mind blowing, right? What is the cause of your cardiac pulsations? Are you directing your cardiac muscle to circulate blood throughout your vascular system? No, right? The functioning of your body is governed by the directives issued by your subconscious faculty.

However, what exactly does the term "subconscious mind" refer to? The region in question pertains to the retention of all one's life experiences within the cerebral cortex. It serves as a repository for all your recollections, abilities, convictions, and values. In addition, it retains a record of every image you have encountered throughout the duration of your life.

To comprehend this concept, let us assume that you are endeavoring to acquire proficiency in the Spanish language. Initially, one may encounter difficulty in expressing oneself fluently in the language. The reason behind this phenomenon is that you continue to utilize your conscious mind during attempts to communicate in the language. However, with consistent practice and increased frequency of Spanish usage, one can effortlessly communicate and comprehend the language. The language has now been stored in your subliminal mind.

The subconscious mind is accountable for the execution of all your involuntary actions and the generation of your emotions. Let us examine a deeply distressing and highly emotional encounter - sexual assault. A woman who experienced sexual abuse in her early years would experience emotions of anger and fear whenever she encounters a portrayal of a rape scene in a film or television program. This is due to the fact that the experience has already been ingrained in her subconscious.

The subconscious mind possesses considerable potency. It possesses the ability to prompt your engagement in activities and evoke emotional responses. However, there is one limitation it possesses - it is incapable of discerning the distinction between a genuine encounter and a mere figment of imagination. This is crazy, right?

Now, let us proceed to examine an illustrative demonstration that resonates with all of us. Suppose, for instance, that you experience a distressing nightmare. You had a dream wherein an individual made an attempt on your life and caused harm to your family. The dream is illusory. However, upon awakening, one experiences involuntary body tremors and profuse perspiration, as if the dream had materialized into reality.

A team of researchers attached electrodes to the muscles of the runners, using a device to gauge their muscular activity. The individuals instructed the runners to follicle their eyelids and visualize themselves participating in a competitive running event. The outcome was unexpected and awe-inspiring. The process of contemplating participation in a race engaged the very muscles employed by the competitors during the actual act of running in said race.

All of our longings, yearnings, and aspirations are encapsulated within the depths of our subconscious realm. And thus, it is an undeniable reality that you are inclined to attract whatever you retain within the depths of your subconscious mind. Please engage in the following exercise: for a duration of five minutes per day, over the course of seven days, kindly close your eyes and concentrate on visualizing a car of the color purple. After the passage of one week, one would begin to observe the presence of purple-colored automobiles on the streets. This is unexpected due to the relatively low prevalence of these automobiles.

Your reality is influenced by the workings of your subconscious mind. However, what influences the formation of the subconscious mind? Essentially, all the factors that influence your mind comprise a broad spectrum encompassing television programs, personal encounters, social circles, educators, academic background, surroundings, and even musical preferences.

In order to leverage the potential of your subconscious mind and attain all desired outcomes in life, it is imperative to immerse yourself in circumstances, ideas, and sentiments that are congruent with your aspirations.

Suppose we generate a total of sixty thousand thoughts within a single day. Regrettably, a majority of these thoughts fall in the realm of negativity, intertwined with emotions of fear, apprehension, remorse, melancholy, and discontentment. These pessimistic thought processes generate an elevation in cortisol, a stress hormone acknowledged for its capacity to induce a range of adverse health conditions. These thoughts also tend to manifest adverse circumstances or occurrences that align with the same unfavorable emotions currently experienced by an individual.

Numerous individuals maintain the belief that anxiety can be attributed to certain circumstances. However, that is not always the situation. Frequently, it is your cognitive patterns that contribute to the onset of depressive or anxious symptoms. It pertains to your psychological reactions towards an adverse situation.

The trajectory of your life is determined by the power of your thoughts. They shape your reality. However, there is a positive aspect to consider - you possess the ability to govern your thoughts, and consequently, exert influence over your forthcoming opportunities.

Allow me to present a methodology wherein you can harness the cognitive faculties of your mind and leverage the principles of the law of attraction, thereby bringing about the materialization of your aspirations in the realm of your lived experience.

Please clearly articulate your desires.

A significant proportion of individuals lack clarity about their aspirations and objectives in life. In order to experience genuine and complete contentment in life, it is imperative to possess a clear understanding of the desires one wishes to actualize. Are you aspiring to excel in the field of law and establish yourself as a accomplished attorney? Are you interested in becoming a phenomenally successful entrepreneur with a net worth in the billions? Would you like to assume both roles? I would advise against considering the desires of your parents. Consider your desired outcome.

When one possesses clarity regarding their desires, it becomes more feasible for the cosmos to align circumstances, possibilities, and individuals capable of facilitating the attainment of their objectives and aspirations.

Direct your attention towards your desired outcome.

Directing your attention towards your desires enhances your vibrational resonance and establishes harmonious alignment with your aspirations. Indeed, it should be noted that all phenomena within our world possess a distinct vibrational quality. This is the underlying cause for the feeling of exhaustion that ensues upon engaging in conversations with individuals who consistently express dissatisfaction. This phenomenon also explains the sense of joy that accompanies the act of planning a journey or discussing one's aspirations.

When one is consistently preoccupied with unfavorable thoughts, one's vibrational frequency lowers. The universe will subsequently operate and manifest circumstances and events that will assist in upholding your existing vibrational state. This is the underlying cause behind the continuous accumulation of unfavorable circumstances when one is in a state of agitation or dissatisfaction.

When one engages in optimistic thinking, they resonate at a frequency aligned with achievement, affluence, and affection. To effectively attract what you desire, it is crucial to maintain unwavering focus and continually contemplate upon it.

Believe.

In order to draw and materialize desired outcomes, it is imperative to possess a firm belief. It is imperative to place your trust in the infinite capacity of the universe to manifest all that your heart yearns for. It is essential to trust and believe. Faith can move mountains. By placing your trust in the universe, you emit a resonant frequency that elevates your being, thereby harmonizing your existence with your desired outcomes.

In order to draw your dreams and aspirations towards yourself, it is imperative to cultivate the belief that you are deserving of them. It is imperative to hold the belief that one is deserving of leading the existence that aligns with their aspirations. In the subsequent sections of this book, you will encounter various instruments that shall fortify your convictions regarding the potent influence exerted by the thoughts in materializing your desires.

The principle of the law of attraction holds substantial potential for manifesting your desired career, your perfect life companion, and even a considerable sum of one million dollars within your financial holdings. However, correct usage is imperative. In the subsequent chapters of this literary work, invaluable techniques of utmost simplicity and efficacy shall be elucidated, enabling you to effortlessly magnetize an array of positive aspects in your life.

The Foundational Principles Of Energy Medicine

Although conventional paradigms are inadequate in explaining these phenomena, it is the anomalies that unveil the deficiencies of a paradigm and contribute to its refinement. There exists no alternative explanation for the cardiac transplantation data that is more coherent than the notion that the heart possesses a field (in actuality, the heart's electrical field is approximately 60 times more potent than that of the brain, while its magnetic field is possibly up to 5000 times stronger, as indicated by certain estimates). It is plausible to assume that this field encompasses information pertaining to the individual in question.

- Reach

Energy medicine has the ability to exert an influence on a wide array of physical conditions, as it is capable of addressing the underlying energetic foundations of biological processes. Energy medicine is focused on optimizing the energetic forces that envelop, penetrate, and sustain the physical framework and operations of the body, including its cellular components, organs, bloodstream, and lymphatic system. This pertains to vital aspects such as the immune response, respiratory function, and cardiovascular health. Energy medicine technologies can exert an influence on the process of gene expression.

Alterations in the patient's energy flow can be effectively targeted through the application of techniques such as holding, tapping, or massaging specific energy points, leading to modifications in the progression of the disease rather than mere symptom alleviation observed in conventional therapies for multiple sclerosis.

- Efficiency

Energy medicine effectively regulates biological mechanisms with precise precision, rapidity, and adaptability. Energy medicine procedures aim at addressing the root causes of both systemic and specific illnesses, transmitting signals significantly faster than chemical signals and enabling prompt and valuable feedback to practitioners, thereby facilitating adjustments to therapies for achieving desired outcomes.

Harmonizing and fortifying the energies encompassing and permeating the heart of an individual recovering from a coronary episode fosters an internal milieu conducive to recuperation and rejuvenation.

- Practicality

Energy medicine facilitates the process of healing and the prevention of illness by employing techniques that are straightforward, cost-effective, and non-intrusive. Energy medicine utilizes precise movements, stances, and manual techniques that do not necessitate advanced technological apparatus and do not yield unforeseen adverse reactions. Evaluating disturbances in the energy flow to a patient's kidneys enables the implementation of nuanced and adaptable treatments, surpassing traditional medical or surgical interventions. Furthermore, this approach holds the potential for preventive measures, thus circumventing potential damage to a vulnerable organ.

- Patient Empowerment

Energy medicine encompasses various self-care methods that individuals can employ within the comfort of their own homes, fostering an enhanced bond between patients and practitioners during the therapeutic journey. Self-administered energy medicine techniques can be employed for the purpose of identifying imbalanced systems, implementing corrective measures, and fostering resilient energy patterns across the entirety of the body. Individuals with cirrhosis may employ regular methods to harmonize the energies that impact the liver and enhance its capacity for recuperation.

- Quantum Compatibility

Energy medicine incorporates non-linear concepts that align with the principles of remote healing, the curative impact of prayer, and the role of intention in the healing process. Energy medicine explores the domains that influence consciousness and operate across time (such as macroscopic quantum interactions), positing potential explanations for the notable outcomes observed in the placebo effect and remote healing, which are tied to desire and anticipation.

Individuals diagnosed with cancer may be instructed in methods that involve harnessing the curative potential of focused intent, as well as being educated on how the thoughts and imagery they cultivate can impact their healing process.

● Holistic Orientation

Energy medicine fosters the integration of the physical, psychological, and spiritual aspects, leading to not only the restoration of health but also enhanced overall wellness, inner calmness, and vitality. Energy medicine is based on the fundamental principle that the interconnectedness of the body, mind, and spirit is essential, and its promotion is paramount.

Individuals afflicted with ulcerative colitis can receive education on the potential impact of psychological conflicts on their symptoms, along with interventions that effectively address the underlying emotional components of these conflicts.

Fundamentally, conventional medicine focuses on the physiological aspects of cells, tissues, and organs. Fundamentally, energy medicine centers its attention on the domains that coordinate and regulate the growth and mending of cells, tissues, and organs, along with methods to exert an impact on such domains.

This confers several advantages upon energy medicine when compared to the conventional medical approach. These characteristics can be regarded as the foundational principles that distinguish energy medicine as a significant breakthrough in the field of healthcare.

● Penetration— Energy medicine has the capacity to influence a wide spectrum of physical ailments as it has the ability to address the underlying energy sources of biological processes. The human body constitutes a dynamic energy system, rather than being solely comprised of its mechanical components. The dermal layer expels approximately 30 photons per square centimeter per second.

All cellular structures generate electromagnetic radiation. All physiological processes are regulated by electrical impulses. In contrast, Western medicine remains focused on the biochemical aspects of the human body, paying limited attention to its energetic and organizational fields, predominantly relying on pharmaceutical and surgical interventions as opposed to energy-based remedies. Nevertheless, contemporary research does not corroborate this unilateral approach. The impact of energy fields on gene expression may indeed reside at the core of energy medicine's substantial effectiveness in treating and preventing even the most enigmatic health ailments. Numerous scientific investigations carried out over the past five decades have consistently indicated that the imperceptible energies within the electromagnetic spectrum exert a substantial impact on all facets of biological regulation. Distinctive electromagnetic radiation patterns govern the processes of DNA, RNA, and protein synthesis, influence alterations in protein conformation and functionality, and exert authority over gene regulation, cellular division, cellular differentiation, and morphogenesis (the mechanism by which cells organize into organs and tissues).

Hormonal excretion, neural development and operation, essentially the foundational mechanisms that greatly contribute to the manifestation of life.

What implications does this lack of consideration for the role of energy in governing biological processes hold for the field of modern medicine? It involves more intrusive procedures that are comparatively less effective in targeting underlying causative processes and less precise in modifying the mechanisms it can influence.

For instance, in cases where the body experiences electromagnetic imbalances prompting the production of chemicals like estrogen or progesterone to reinstate equilibrium, the molecular synthesis occurs with utmost precision and accuracy at the specific site of requirement. Energy therapies designed to augment estrogen or progesterone levels administer electromagnetic impulses to the body, thereby stimulating the body's innate mechanisms to produce the necessary hormones.

How To Approach The Throne Of Grace For Answers

SEEK HIS FACE

Subsequently, you shall earnestly pursue the presence of the Lord your God, and you shall indeed encounter Him when you wholeheartedly and fervently undertake the quest. In times of hardship, when adversity befalls you, in the future days you shall seek solace in the Lord your God and heed His divine counsel. Indeed, the compassionate nature of the Lord your God is unwavering, as He shall never forsake, eradicate, or disregard the covenant made with your forefathers, as He solemnly pledged to them..." Deuteronomy 4:29-31.

One must initially endeavor to achieve exceptional spiritual communion with heaven by diligently pursuing the countenance of the divine through fervent supplication. This pursuit is catalyzed by the act of humbling oneself before the Almighty and beseeching His favor in the revered name of His son, Jesus. The virtue of humility is crucial; David displayed humility before him and achieved remarkable outcomes, gaining extraordinary results and triumphs beyond his expectations.

Moses was instilling a sense of encouragement in the children of God, emphasizing the certainty of finding the divine presence upon diligent pursuit. The divine presence is not concealed, and once the desire to seek divine intervention and test its efficacy arises within you, it shall be promptly granted.

Recall the biblical account wherein individuals, similar to the woman who suffered from a chronic blood disorder for a span of twelve years, fervently pursued Jesus with a humble and resolute spirit. They fervently sought to merely touch the hem of Jesus' garment, fully convinced that such an act would lead to their restoration of sound health. In Matthew 9:20-22, Mark 5:25-34, and Luke 8:43-48, we encounter Zacchaeus, a Tax Collector of considerable affluence and influence. Expressing great humility, he ascended a nearby tree in order to catch a glimpse of Jesus. This solitary deed served as the catalyst for a profound miracle of salvation, profoundly impacting both his own life and that of his family. This outcome was unprecedented in his life, as he had not anticipated it. However, the humbled spirit ushered it forth into his existence. In the scripture passage of Luke 19:1-10, it is recounted that Nicodemus, a member of the Pharisees and a prominent leader among the Jewish community, became aware of Jesus' sentiments towards the Pharisees and Sadducees. This awareness on the part of Nicodemus led to a notable response from Jesus, one characterized by humility. John 3:1-21.

In the presence of humility, one shall perpetually behold the manifestation of the divine and witness extraordinary interventions that will elicit amazement and wonder.

Though the LORD is highly esteemed, he regards the humble with benevolence; despite his lofty position, he observes them from a distance...Psalm 138:6"

One can attain spiritual connection with God during times of distress by demonstrating humble devotion. Subsequently, you will attain exceptional proximity to his benevolent authority and engender a profound manifestation of his omnipotence in your existence.

PRAYER POINTS

a) Seek the development of a spirit of humility

b) Kindly beseech the Lord to graciously illuminate you with his presence at this moment.

c) Humble yourself before the Lord and request His presence in a renewed manner

d) Seek divine intervention for the manifestation of abundant blessings from above.

e) Kindly request for him to grant you the ability to perceive his presence through a deepened sense of understanding.

f) Kindly petition him for the favor of enabling the actualization of your aspirations as you earnestly pursue his divine presence.

g) Request his permission to have the honor of utilizing his angelic abilities for your benefit.

Pursue the presence of the Divine Being with a heart full of gratitude

Do not live in a state of distress over anything, rather, in every circumstance, approach God through prayer and supplication, expressing gratitude as you present your needs. Furthermore, the tranquility bestowed by God, surpassing comprehension, shall shield the depths of your hearts and intellect in the presence of Christ Jesus...Philippians 4:6-7"

God is moved when individuals approach his presence with gratitude, regardless of the adversities they may be encountering. Approaching God with a mindset characterized by unwavering faith in His ability to provide solutions to your problems or fulfill your needs has a profoundly profound impact on how God perceives and responds to you. The centurion approached Jesus with a conviction that by simply uttering a single word, his servant would be completely healed... Matthew 8:5-13.

The scripture articulates that this must be the case in every circumstance, regardless of the severity of said circumstance.

Jesus was preparing to bring Lazarus back to life after he had been interred in the sepulcher for a duration of four days... According to John 11:17, he expressed his gratitude towards God. This is an indication that when you keep thanking God in your challenges and difficulties, he will answer you and honor his name in that situation.

Expressing gratitude to the divine signifies acknowledging God as one's savior and redeemer. It also signifies acknowledging God as the ultimate source of reliance and expressing gratitude for the opportunity to seek his assistance.

PRAYER POINTS

a) earnestly beseech for a heart filled with gratitude

b) Seek a heart that exhibits unwavering trust in divine power.

c) Request divine illumination regarding the enigmatic aspects of the spiritual realm, so as to perpetually comprehend and deeply value the essence of God.

d) Seek for his benevolence through heartfelt prayers

e) Entreat for the pleasure derived from achieving one's goals upon approaching his divine seat of benevolence.

How Visualization Works

Gaining knowledge of the mechanics behind visualization enhances one's ability to engage in more effective visualization techniques. Implementing a method without thoughtful consideration may fail to produce the intended outcomes.

How It Works

The human psyche is comprised of two distinct components: the conscious mind and the subconscious mind. We engage in conscious or rational thought, and any thoughts that are recurrent become embedded in our subconscious or creative mind. The subconscious mind can be likened to a computational system. It lacks autonomous thinking capabilities and discernment skills to distinguish between morally sound and unsound, as well as accurate and misleading information. It accepts and considers at face value, whatever is presented to it.

When the cognizant mind repeatedly imparts the equivalent idea to the subconscious, it initiates regarding the thought with gravity and commences efforts to manifest it.

The experiences of our lives are stored within the realms of the subconscious, which has the ability to access them. It also possesses the ability to tap into the Universal consciousness, where no concept is beyond reach.

The subconscious mind subsequently triggers circumstances in which our recurring thoughts are materialized.

I previously encountered a narrative that effectively illustrates the remarkable impact of visualization, albeit through a negative lens. Therefore, exercise caution in the inquiries you make. You might get it.')

A gentleman had a daughter who was afflicted with severe arthritis. He made concerted efforts to explore various medicines, yet achieved no discernible outcome. Whenever he encountered someone, he would often express his strong desire to find a remedy for his daughter, stating, "I would be willing to sacrifice my own limb for her recovery." While he used this expression metaphorically, he continued to repeat it on numerous occasions.

Curiously, several years hence, whilst engaging in automobile travel, he encountered an unfortunate incident whereby his right appendage was forcefully severed from his physical form. Within a short span of time, his daughter's arthritis was completely healed.

To gain a comprehensive understanding of the functioning of visualization, it is imperative that we acknowledge the primary form of communication utilized by the subconscious mind is visual representation.

Although it exhibits equal proficiency in word translation, it is more susceptible to influence by visual representations. Hence, the efficacy of visualization lies in its ability to prompt the subconscious to manifest one's desires.

It is equally imperative to focus solely on the ultimate outcome rather than the process involved. We must only convey to the subconscious the desired information. Allow the subconscious to determine the methodology for obtaining it.

An image possesses the capacity to convey a magnitude of meaning equivalent to that of a thousand words. We are all familiar with that statement already! This assertion holds particularly true when it comes to the effective application of visualization.

Visualization is an efficacious instrument for addressing the ailment and infirmity that may manifest in your existence. Visualization, an introspective practice, employs visual depictions or imagery to harmonize the mind and promote the restoration of our physical well-being. The cerebral hemisphere is anatomically partitioned into a left hemisphere responsible for logical functions and a right hemisphere that governs creative processes. The majority of our existence is dedicated to employing the left hemisphere of the brain, which is associated with logic and rationality. Through the application of visualization techniques, we engage our inherent capacity for creativity and achieve a harmonious equilibrium between the hemispheres of our brain. This equilibrium nurtures the inherent healing mechanisms of the psyche and physique.

Visualization employs imagery to modify one's emotional state, thereby prompting changes in one's feelings that ultimately manifest as physical sensations capable of alleviating or eliminating symptoms.

The cognitive aspect of the human psyche is manifested as emotion, which consequently engenders feelings. The corporeal manifestation of the human anatomy is synonymous with perception. When an emotion arises, it gives rise to a sensation that manifests in a physical manner. Visualization provides the brain with constructive mental images that elicit shifts in emotions, giving rise to a sensory experience.

This is the method by which one can access their mind-body connection.

Frequently, we engage in the logical and analytical processes of our brain to ensure our survival. This engenders a disturbance in cerebral equilibrium. By yielding to our right hemisphere, we tap into the intricate connection between mind and body, thus restoring equilibrium within the brain and facilitating a state of receptivity to transformation and revitalization.

Research has indicated that negative emotions have a detrimental effect on our immune system and hinder our mental well-being. Experiencing adverse emotions hinders and impedes our progress towards attaining our objectives, thereby inhibiting the cognitive functions necessary for realizing our desired outcomes. Positive emotions significantly enhance the functioning of the immune system and promote a state of cognitive equilibrium that fosters adaptability.

The procedure for visualization is straightforward.

1) Seek out a serene environment. 2) Discover a tranquil location. 3) Locate a peaceful setting. 4) Identify a quiet spot. 5) Ascertain a restful place.

2) Clearly articulate your purpose.

3) Place your focus on the inhalation and exhalation of your breath.

4) Start your visualization. The process of visualization typically requires several weeks to yield results, and it is advisable to engage in it both in the

morning and at nighttime prior to sleeping.

A significant number of individuals experience positive outcomes following their initial attempt. In order to achieve a favorable result, it is imperative to elucidate the precise nature of your intention and cultivate a profound recognition, acceptance, and faith in its viability. In fact, it is crucial to possess an unwavering certainty that it has already been successful, surpassing any plausible doubt.

Humility Serves As The Yardstick For Measuring Spiritual Achievement.

Humility constitutes a state of mind, and it is incumbent upon one to recognize that prior to bestowing anything upon an individual, God will thoroughly scrutinize their thoughts and intents. One can observe an individual of limited means and perceive them as being exceptionally modest, although such assumptions may not invariably hold true. This could occasionally be attributed to a limited range of alternatives. Therefore, it cannot be deduced that an individual possesses humility, as their true character will only be revealed when their circumstances evolve. Therefore, the divine Father, whose paradigm differs from our terrestrial framework, will assess the modesty of His disciples.

Kindly peruse this remarkable scriptural passage on the pious modesty demonstrated by the esteemed figure,

Lord Jesus Christ, as documented within the pages of...

Philippians 2:6 He, who possessed the essence of divinity, did not view it as an act of theft or wrongfulness to be on par with God. 7 Instead, he willingly relinquished his esteemed status and assumed the role of a servant, adopting the likeness of humanity. 8 Thus, appearing in the manner of a mortal, he demonstrated great humility, obediently accepting death, even the most agonizing one on the cross. (KJV)

When we observe the figure of the Lord Jesus Christ, we witness a profound embodiment of humility as an exemplary paragon. According to the scripture, the divine Father and His Son, Jesus Christ, existed in mutual existence throughout the boundless expanse of eternity. The biblical text of Hebrews 2:9 conveys that Jesus demonstrated deep humility by assuming a position subordinate to that of the angels, and by taking on the form and resemblance of mankind. You might lack comprehension regarding the actions undertaken by Him, yet it can be affirmed that His sacrifice holds profound favorability in the divine realm.

Let us examine this matter from a divine vantage point. Angelic entities are perpetual celestial beings dedicated to the administration and provision of service to the divine deity. I would like to convey the idea that Angels function as obedient individuals within the realm of God's kingdom. According to the testimony of David in Psalm 8:4, angels are also depicted as occupying a superior position to that of human beings. Therefore, upon Jesus' determination to humble Himself in the realm of heaven, to the degree where He assumed the appearance and characteristics of humanity. This exemplifies the modesty displayed by the Lord Jesus Christ. Deliberately relinquishing his splendor, dignity, and elevated status, he descended into the earthly realm with the purpose of reconciling the estranged offspring of God back to His presence.

You shall recall the act of treason committed by Adam, for which there existed no alternative means of satisfying the ensuing liabilities apart from the redemption offered through the person of Jesus Christ. Consequently, when summoned by divine decree to assume a mortal existence, with the purpose of effectuating the salvation of mankind, he willingly embraced this responsibility, undertaking it with utmost delight. This act performed by Jesus Christ stands as the most remarkable manifestation of his devotion to God the Father and his benevolence towards humanity. Presently, the divine Creator has bestowed a distinct response to manifest His genuine appreciation for the Lord Jesus Christ's dutifulness and selfless acts.

Let us examine the Scriptures regarding the divine endorsement bestowed upon the labor of Jesus Christ by the heavenly

Father. Our attention is directed towards Philippians 2:9, which states that God has magnified Jesus and bestowed upon him a name that surpasses all others. Verse 10 further explains that every knee shall bow at the mention of Jesus, be it beings in heaven, on earth, or below the earth. Verse 11 also emphasizes that every tongue shall acknowledge Jesus Christ as the Lord, ultimately bringing glory to God the Father. (KJV)

Esteemed reader, I implore you to peruse it at your own leisure. The Lord Jesus Christ has been bestowed with the utmost power and authority by the Divine Supreme Being. Jesus Christ has been bestowed with a name that surpasses all others in prestige and dignity to such an extent that upon utterance of said name, every entity in the celestial realm, earthly domain, and subterranean depths should humbly bend their knees in reverence. This demonstrates great strength; do you perceive the profound impact that humility has had upon Jesus? He has been bestowed with a name that holds sway over the realms of heaven, earth, and the underworld, impervious to any resistance. This esteemed distinction is bestowed eternally upon Jesus for all of eternity.

It is truly remarkable to witness individuals from various corners of the globe devoting themselves to the worship and service of God, specifically through the veneration of Jesus Christ. Allow me to inquire, did Jesus attain such a distinction through adeptly navigating the realm of politics? The bestowment of this formidable appellation upon him by God did not arise from his extraordinary oratorical skills; rather, it was bestowed upon him solely due to his unwavering humility. The most optimal approach to obtain power, authority, and anointing from God involves mastering the art of being submissive to God.

If such a standard of humility was deemed appropriate for the Son of God himself, it is incumbent upon us to likewise emulate the pattern set by Jesus Christ. He epitomized the ideal model that has been presented to us, and if we emulate Jesus's example by cultivating humility in our relationship with God, we can anticipate that God will bestow honor upon us and employ us for endeavors beyond our imagination or contemplation. God's criterion for elevating individuals involves the virtue of humility, which is most exemplified in the divine anointing and exaltation of Jesus Christ.

Please refer to Numbers 12:3, wherein it is stated that Moses was exemplarily humble, surpassing all individuals in his modesty among the inhabitants of the earth. (ISV)

Dear esteemed individuals, let us engage in the enlightened pursuit of reading and explicating the life and teachings of Moses, an esteemed prophet who holds an esteemed place within the pages of the Old Testament. This individual named Moses is documented to have possessed the virtue of humility, as attested by the account written about him, which describes him as being the most humble individual of his era. This statement may prove to be significantly arduous for each individual reading this book to comprehend and acknowledge as verifiable. However, it is a factual statement that remains unchallenged and irrefutable. Undoubtedly, Moses displayed remarkable humility; however, the people of Israel failed to comprehend his true character. I intend to provide further clarification on this matter in order to enhance your understanding.

Upon the departure of the Children of Israel from Egypt, under the guidance of Moses, a prevailing belief among the majority was that Moses harbored intentions of assuming a position of kingship or rulership over them. Consequently, a faction of individuals rose in rebellion against the authority of Moses. This occurrence captured the notice of the Divine Being. Therefore, it was predetermined by God to bring about the obliteration of the entire nation of Israel in order to cultivate a subsequent generation under the guidance of Moses (Deuteronomy 9:13-14). The conduct exhibited by the individuals caused a great displeasure to God, as it was evident that they lacked comprehension regarding the judgment of Moses.

Due to Moses' intervention, God exhibited appreciation for his humility, recognizing that Moses was not motivated by personal gain when leading the nation of Israel. He attained a revered status throughout the Bible, and we commemorate him as a paragon of unwavering faith. A key factor in the ability of Jesus, Moses, and numerous individuals to experience the blessings of God lies in their embodiment of humility.

The demonstration of God's consistent tendency to bestow His ability and power upon individuals who dedicate themselves to His service arises, on the condition that they cultivate the virtue of humility. It is imperative to bear in mind that humility is a state of mind, and thus, God will discern our thoughts and intentions in order to ascertain whether we are worthy of His presence or not. Nevertheless, modesty has emerged as a distinctive attribute that delineated the triumph of influential individuals in the realm of divine service. Through practical knowledge and adherence to authority, we have come to acknowledge that profound and influential demonstrations of the divine can be witnessed when individuals in positions of leadership demonstrate a profound sense of modesty and when religious congregations embrace and embody the virtue of humility.

What is the anticipated timeframe for the realization of my manifestation?

Individuals often exhibit exaggerated reactions when their aspirations require an extended period to materialize, as they hold the conviction that there is no rationale in striving towards goals that necessitate a prolonged timeframe for realization. It is simply a futile utilization of their time.

In order to achieve success, one must be patient and seize the opportune moment. One cannot merely select a moment and instantaneously manifest their aspirations. All events occur at the appropriate moment. Irrespective of one's belief, such is the inherent essence of existence. You are obligated to address this matter irrespective of any circumstances.

Certain individuals experience feelings of frustration as they await the fulfillment of their ambitions, which can be attributed to a deficiency in forbearance. A significantly large proportion of individuals who aspire to accomplish a specific life objective express a preference for expeditious achievement.

Manifestation entails a progressive journey characterized by procedural steps, signifying that the attainment of your objectives may require a considerable span of time. In order to comprehend appropriate conduct within the given situation, it is imperative to possess a receptive mindset and engage in introspection regarding the underlying reasons for your failure to attain your goals. There exist a multitude of factors that could potentially impact the process of manifestation. The possibilities are manifold, but it is advisable to endeavor to ascertain its nature.

An alternative approach for handling the situation is to maintain composure. Frustration should not be the preferred recourse, regardless of the complexity of the matter at hand. It will only exacerbate the issue and is unlikely to aid you in achieving your objectives. Although approaching the issue with anger might offer momentary respite, it will not effectively rectify the problem.

In the event that you encounter a complicated situation, it could potentially serve as an assessment of your composure. Thus, by approaching it with a positive outlook, you will find that managing it will not pose any significant challenges.

For certain individuals, the act of manifesting proves to be an arduous endeavor. This is due to the fact that not every individual possesses the fortitude necessary to confront the aspects that evoke fear within them. There exist numerous impediments to manifestation that inhibit a significant portion of individuals from attaining their desires. Hence, certain individuals refrain from endeavoring to actualize their desires or persistently struggle to bring about the fruition of their aspirations in their everyday existence.

This implies that individuals hold diverse perspectives on a given matter, which can vary depending on their reactions to and interpretations of environmental stimuli. Fear is a prevalent hindrance that often manifests itself in various ways. Numerous individuals harbor a profound sense of dread towards any potential disruptions to their livelihood. They engage in such behavior due to a multitude of factors. Certain individuals may have experienced setbacks or lack of success when endeavoring to change their overarching life goals or aspirations.

The majority of individuals who aspire to manifest often contend with the challenge of fear. Certain individuals assert that they perpetually experience apprehension regarding the outcomes, harboring an aversion towards perceiving themselves as inadequate. Despite facing failures in the past, numerous individuals who have achieved success have utilized their setbacks as a driving force to attain their aspirations in life.

To achieve the realization of something, one must exercise caution and consider the potential ramifications of their decisions. It is imperative that you refrain from limiting your perspective and instead persevere in actualizing your ambitions, for they are the fundamental components of acquiring proficiency in manifestation and attaining success in the days to come.

In addition, it is imperative that you maintain a willingness to be receptive to guidance or suggestions from others, as they have the potential to significantly contribute to the collaborative pursuit of your life objectives. It is essential to bear in mind the prescribed guidelines and precautions of manifestation, so as to remain cognizant of the vital elements that may steer you towards the correct path.

The Magic Of Manifesting

Manifestation is not akin to the illusory practices witnessed in circus acts. It does not involve any form of deceptive manipulation or a mere demonstration of telepathic abilities typically showcased at social gatherings for entertainment purposes. The act of manifestation is a straightforward undertaking, albeit one that necessitates establishing a profound rapport with the cosmic forces in order to bring it to fruition in one's existence. Manifestation, in more erudite language, can be described as the act of articulating one's desires and needs, subsequently relinquishing control over the request, thereby allowing the desired outcome to materialize. Expressed in such fashion may appear uncomplicated, however, it is a nuanced undertaking. The human brain possesses inherent neural pathways that empower it to assume autonomous control and independently rectify various situations. This aspect of our brain's functioning represents an innate survival mechanism deeply ingrained within us since ancient times. Consequently, altering or easing this state of mind is an arduous and challenging task. Once you attain a comprehensive understanding of the obstacles that hinder the fulfillment of your aspirations, you can commence the process of overcoming these vexing impediments and progress towards the extraordinary possibilities that eagerly await realization.

If the process of manifestation possessed inherent simplicity, all individuals would find themselves devoid of desires and necessities, leading to the creation of an idyllic world. Although it would be desirable to envision a future where such progress is attained, it is disheartening to acknowledge that numerous individuals remain unwilling to relinquish their authority and dominance over others or possessions, primarily due to their conviction that no one or nothing else could surpass their capabilities. The act of manifestation does not provide an unequivocal assurance of immense affluence and opulence. Rather, it bestows upon individuals a sense of tranquility, contentment, harmonious connection with their surroundings, and a deeper understanding of their own being. It may provide you with prosperity, as circumstances warrant, along with numerous other facets, yet the cosmos serves as an expansive reservoir of benefits that manifest in diverse manners, and wealth encompasses multifaceted interpretations. The cosmic forces often exhibit a peculiar sense of irony when determining the allocation of one's possessions or circumstances. If one manages to establish a connection with that power, they will acquire the ability to embrace the cosmic humor, even in situations where circumstances do not align precisely with their expectations, and develop a genuine appreciation for things as they truly are.

If one does not possess a proper sense of gratitude for the possessions they currently possess, what incentive does the universe have to grant them additional possessions which would also be undervalued?

If you are genuinely capable of acknowledging and cherishing your existing possessions, and if you are willing to invest the necessary effort to establish a profound bond with the forces governing the cosmos, what we shall refer to as a state of unity, then when you extend a plea for anything, the universe should have no valid grounds for denying your request. Occasionally, however, we articulate solicitations that are not aligned with genuine necessities, and in turn, the universe reciprocates with contrasting outcomes. Occasionally, the outcome surpasses our initial expectations, presenting us with something of superior quality, allowing us to readily perceive the miraculous nature of the situation. Upon receiving something unexpected, individuals often have a tendency to assume that their request has been rejected or disregarded, without fully grasping the possibility that what they desire may not align with their own welfare.

The universe will intervene and rectify our actions when we deviate from acceptable norms and fail to align with the principles of nature and its governing laws. When an error occurs due to lack of knowledge, the universe tends to offer lenient admonishment. Nonetheless, if the error is severe and deliberate, with the aim of causing harm to someone or something, the cosmic forces generally choose to sever our bonds with the interconnectedness, enabling us to experience the consequences of our own unsightly human disposition. Greed, being the most repulsive aspect of human nature, fundamentally contradicts the principle of unity. Oneness is a willingness to give what you have to another so that all may feel peace and comfort, not a desire to have the biggest and best of everything while others suffer with nothing at all. Hence, should you possess an inclination to employ the practice of manifesting for your own individual advantage, you may proceed to experiment with it. However, I prefer not to be in close proximity to you when the universe presents its repercussions.

When utilized appropriately, the act of manifesting can yield numerous positive outcomes. When an individual sincerely petitions the universe for an essential resource, apprehensive of alternative means of acquisition, it is indeed a wondrous occurrence when said item materializes discreetly at their residence within a matter of days. It is truly enchanting when what you have requested is bestowed upon you, surpassing your initial expectations and adorned with enhancements. Manifestation is often likened to the act of prayer, wherein individuals make supplications and anticipate a response to their entreaties. Manifestation entails a distinct variation, whereby upon attaining a profound harmony with the universe, one becomes capable of subconsciously contemplating a desire or necessity. One may choose to dismiss the matter as a fleeting idea, and soon thereafter, the coveted object will materialize before one's eyes. Due to our society's tendency to require empirical evidence before accepting ideas, it is necessary for you to initiate the procedure through a systematic approach of trial and error, wherein you make deliberate appeals to the universe for the precise resources you require. I use the term "trial and error" as it is highly probable that you will encounter initial errors or missteps in expressing your requirements. Please bear in mind that the universe possesses its own brand of comedic essence that may not consistently align with your personal sense of humor, though it should nevertheless evoke a smile from you. As an illustration, the outcome of your car request could encompass a spectrum of possibilities, ranging from a postcard adorned with an image of a car, to a miniature replica, all the way to an actual motor vehicle. It is as though the cosmos is inquiring, "What exactly was your true desire?" and engages in playful manipulation.

When formulating those initial requests, it is prudent to consider the nature of your appeal and its underlying rationale. Kindly provide details in your request, if feasible, and demonstrate heartfelt sincerity. The cosmic forces possess inherent knowledge of this fact, however, at times, it may appear as though they are inclined to assess one's integrity. Subsequently, as the spiritual connection between you and your higher power deepens, you may experience instances where you unknowingly make petitions and are subsequently pleasantly surprised by unexpected manifestations. That is the authentic enchantment and marvel of manifestation. Manifestation is a universal ability that transcends the constraints of location, time, and scope, as long as one possesses a profound alignment with the cosmic forces.

The Enigma Behind The Principle Of Attraction

What the intellect can envision, it has the capabilities to accomplish.

This quotation contains significant significance and insightful knowledge. This echoes the teachings of Buddha from millennia ago, who proclaimed, 'You are what you think.'

Both quotations fundamentally address the potency of the human intellect, which serves as a universally accessible instrument for attaining our aspirations. Nevertheless, it is disheartening that numerous individuals frequently overlook this invaluable resource.

Your intellectual capacity harbors profound influence and has the potential to materialize any desired outcome. However, in order to manifest such outcomes, it is imperative that you direct your attention towards the appropriate objectives. This is the point at which the Letter of Agreement fulfills its purpose; hence, let us delve more extensively into it in order to gain a more comprehensive understanding.

The Fundamental Principles of the Law of Attraction

Familiarity with the concept of the Law of Attraction implies an understanding of the idiom 'like attracts like'. It pertains to your capacity to draw towards you all that you earnestly concentrate on in your existence. It represents one of the fundamental principles that govern the ability to utilize the faculties of one's mind to effectively decipher the encoded message inherent in our thoughts, subsequently manifesting it into tangible form. The present condition of your life serves as a reflection of your thoughts, implying that all your accomplishments can be attributed to the influence of your thoughts.

As per the Law of Attraction (LOA), one has the potential to attain any desired outcome envisioning it in the realm of one's mental imagery. If a mental image is vividly perceived and unwaveringly regarded as the ultimate verity, resolute concentration upon it shall inevitably lead to its realization.

For an enhanced comprehension, it is imperative to grasp the functioning of your mind.

What is the Mechanism behind the Law of Attraction?

Regrettably, there is a lack of awareness among a significant portion of individuals regarding the profound impact that the Law of Attraction has on our daily lives. Consciously or unconsciously (primarily unconsciously), each instant in our existence entails our role as human magnets, projecting our emotions, sensations, and thoughts into the universe, thereby drawing closer to us an abundance of what we emit.

All phenomena within the vast expanse of the universe, including the workings of our own cognitive processes, operate at distinct frequencies and exhibit perpetual oscillation. As we engage in cognitive processes, our thoughts emanate into the vast expanse of the universe, perpetually resonating at a specific frequency. In the vast expanse of the cosmos, one encounters an array of analogous and disparate ideas. Given the convergence of comparable phenomena at a relatively consistent frequency, our cognitive inclination tends to gravitate towards congruent thoughts, sentiments, and emotions. This is how similar thoughts gravitate towards one another.

These congruent ideas subsequently convene in a collective grouping, engaging in reciprocal discourse before converging back to their origin. Your cogitation subsequently attracts analogous cognitions, thus encompassing the associated array of experiences, opportunities, concepts, and individuals. Should you happen to encounter an individual who shares the same fervor for literature, feline companions, and the indulgence in caffeinated beverages as you do within the confines of a book club that you presently find yourself in, it would not be a mere coincidence; rather, it is the result of your very own thoughts materializing and shaping your current circumstances.

It is crucial to acknowledge that you exclusively attract those elements towards yourself that you conscientiously and fervently concentrate on. Typically, the human mind generates an estimated range of 50,000 to 70,000 thoughts per day; however, it is important to acknowledge that not every thought manifests itself as a tangible reality. Indeed, a significant number of these thoughts are effectively screened by the RAS (Reticular Activating System) in order to prevent your brain from experiencing excessive informational burden.

The reticular activating system selectively screens and excludes thoughts perceived by the subconscious mind as inconsequential. Several factors contribute to its evaluation process, with two significant determinants being one's degree of concentration and emotional engagement towards a particular thought, sensation, or event. If one nurtures emotional attachment to a thought and dedicates repetitive contemplation to it, one reinforces the connection with it. The concept subsequently attracts additional thoughts resonating at a comparable frequency, resulting in encounters with individuals, experiences, and opportunities that facilitate the manifestation of your ideas.

Positive Thinking Attracts Favorable Opportunities "

The concept of the Law of Attraction is the foundation for the prevailing advice to cultivate a positive mindset, as our thoughts possess a magnetic quality that attracts corresponding experiences into our lives, ultimately shaping our perceived reality. We possess substantial untapped potential residing within our cognitive faculties, readily accessible and unlockable. Yet, due to our lack of awareness, we fail to harness this potential.

One of the primary factors contributing to this issue is the absence of vigilance in monitoring our thoughts and emotions. We inadvertently engage in unfocused ideation, cling to superfluous sentiments, and excessively ruminate without justification, subsequently bemoaning the inexplicable attraction of negativity within our lives.

In order to maintain optimal physical well-being, cultivate inner contentment, enjoy the company of cherished individuals, discover a compatible life partner, excel in one's career endeavors, and experience substantial personal growth, it is imperative to adopt a positive mindset, exercise vigilance over one's thoughts and emotions, and possess a crystallized understanding of one's desires to effectively transmit the appropriate intentions to the cosmos and attract favorable circumstances.

Napoleon Hill, in his literary work entitled 'Think and Grow Rich', recounts the tale of his son who was born with a permanent hearing impairment. The physicians clearly conveyed that he would perpetually lack the ability to perceive sound, and that no therapeutic alternatives existed to remedy his condition.

Napoleon Hill, on the other hand, staunchly rejected this notion and, in his search for efficacious remedies to address the problem, commenced transmitting potent thoughts into the cosmos with unwavering concentration on the same matter. On a daily basis, as bedtime approached, Hill would instill a suggestion into the mind of his son, focusing on his son's ability to perceive auditory stimuli and maintain a robust auditory faculty, simply through verbal communication.

These recommendations assisted in the transformation of Hill's son into a poised and determined young man, regardless of his disability. He consistently rose to challenges and confronted adversities with unwavering resolve. Ultimately, after an extended period of time, Hill and his son were presented with a therapeutic alternative that effectively alleviated his son's auditory deficiency, thus realizing their long-held aspiration. Amidst the bewilderment that gripped the audience, Hill remained resolute in his conviction, attributing this outcome to his unwavering faith in the immense potential harbored within the subconscious mind as well as the profound influence of the law of attraction. The Law of Attraction possesses significant potency, and fortunately, it can be readily harnessed.

Allow us to proceed to the initial measure you must undertake in order to achieve that.

Give It Your Best

Regardless of your aspirations in life, the pivotal aspect is to consistently exert your utmost effort. If you adhere to this advice, you will discover a significant increase in your level of success. Consider the matter, for when exerting maximum effort, you are undoubtedly bound to achieve a greater extent of success. Suppose you possess aptitude in mathematics, tailoring, or the various fields of craftsmanship. Have you ever experienced such fatigue, weariness, frustration, or emotional distress that it hindered your proficiency in that particular skill? Due to the presence of those emotions, you were unable to muster the complete extent of your abilities, thereby leading to a decline in the end result. Hence, it is imperative to ascertain that one is enhancing their intentions.

When one exerts utmost efforts and dedication, the results are undoubtedly conspicuous. It will be evident to all observers that you have made exhaustive efforts. Your supervisor will be aware of the extensive effort you have dedicated. Your friends and family will recognize your diligent efforts in striving for excellence. When you consistently apply maximum effort, you will surpass all other methods. Assume you possess limited proficiency in the culinary arts, yet resolve to undertake the task of preparing a meal. If you approach it with insufficient commitment, the outcome may not be of exceptional quality. In the event that you opt to exert utmost effort, you will adhere more closely to the provided instructions and diligently attend to the meal. It is more probable that the outcome will yield favorable results.

Contemplate all of these aspects and reflect upon the considerable improvements that can be achieved by wholeheartedly employing your capabilities and exerting effort consistently throughout the duration of the day and the entire undertaking. An individual who achieves victory will consistently approach their upcoming task with utmost dedication and exert all their efforts right from the outset. They will only find contentment when they dedicate their utmost effort and resources to every assignment.

Manifestation Of Happiness

This can be easily demonstrated. It is imperative that you assess and reflect upon your own conduct. Once more, envision yourself positioned upon that stone within the midst of a swiftly flowing river. You must make a determination about the direction you desire your life to take. You have the option to either progress towards the next milestone on your path to success or remain stagnant and anticipate no progress. A simple shift in perspective is all that is needed to activate the Law of Attraction.

What types of individuals are drawn to individuals who are content?
What traits are commonly exhibited by individuals who experience happiness?
What is the typical response of individuals who experience happiness towards others?

There is a notable prevalence of individuals who hold the belief that their happiness can be attained through external sources. If one is devoid of self-contentment, reliance on others to achieve lasting happiness is futile and can only offer transient solace. Your character is negative. The manifestation of your happiness is only visible in the presence of another individual providing support. I have information to share with you. It is incumbent upon you to discover internal contentment if you desire enduring happiness. Indeed, it is possible for you to find happiness with another individual; nevertheless, it is essential not to rely on their approval as a prerequisite for your own happiness. You should possess the capabilities to accomplish that task independently.

Many individuals often embark on a quest for an ideal life partner, commonly referred to as "Mr. Right," without first cultivating a solid personal understanding and self-acceptance. In a previous section of the book, I made reference to women who tend to draw in abusive partners. It is not a matter of them being the unfortunate individuals. It pertains to their perspective on life. Typically, individuals who find themselves in such relationships have previously exhibited their own deficiencies. It is conceivable that they are experiencing self-esteem concerns. It is possible that they lack a substantial amount of self-assurance. The issue with attempting to find happiness by relying on another person in circumstances like these is that you are prone to committing significant errors. You enter into relationships where you relinquish the authority to determine your own happiness to your partner, a habit that has been proven to be highly detrimental and inefficient in the pursuit of genuine happiness.

Discovering inner contentment is what facilitates the Law of Attraction to operate in your favor as opposed to being a hindrance. If one perceives oneself as flawed or lacking, one will inevitably draw towards oneself individuals who are likewise flawed or lacking, resulting in a potential for harm. Accordingly, it is logical to initially focus on self-discovery and the manner in which you project your identity. The matter of one's gender is inconsequential, as this principle is applicable without exception. If you convey excessive dependency, you will inevitably appeal to individuals with a penchant for exerting dominance over those who are reliant. Nevertheless, if one faces life with the awareness of being inherently content and self-sufficient, one inadvertently draws in individuals who share this state of perfect happiness and sufficiency. The Law of Attraction is a fundamental principle that holds great importance in achieving desired outcomes in one's life, necessitating the disciplined cultivation of the mind to manifest one's desired identity. During adolescence, individuals commonly grapple with this challenge until they reach the point where they are sufficiently mature and accountable to establish relationships smoothly.

Nevertheless, a significant proportion of children and adolescents in modern times originate from households that have experienced familial dissolution. Currently, half of marriages end in divorce, leading to the unfortunate circumstance where half of the children raised in these households already encounter emotional challenges prior to entering adulthood. It is indeed an arduous concept that necessitates acceptance, yet it is essential that you diligently navigate your own identity and purpose. Employing a vision board can prove advantageous in this endeavor.

Manifesting Happiness

Do you believe that individuals who exhibit positivity and inner fulfillment will be drawn to your presence even if your outward demeanor does not reflect happiness? It is highly unlikely that they will not. If you are perusing these pages, it is likely that you have already arrived at the determination to dedicate effort towards elevating your overall state of contentment, with the intention of experiencing enhanced daily well-being and effectuating positive transformations in your life. Employ your vision board as a platform to document all the positive attributes you deem yourself possessing, and incorporate the qualities you aspire to embody, such as happiness, positivity, amiability, independent thinking, and being good company. Then, sit back from your vision board and close your eyes, imagining yourself to BE that person who will attract positive energy into his or her life. You have the capability to accomplish this task independently and as you spend more time in front of that board, actively reinforcing your own sense of contentment, you will experience an increased level of happiness. Welcome the world with a pleasant countenance. Cease perceiving the cup as being half empty and eliminate any deficiency in your trust towards life. One cannot establish a fulfilling relationship while harboring internal negativity. Maintaining a positive outlook towards the world, diligently rehearsing in front of your vision board each day, adeptly nurturing a mindset of contentment and happiness, and swiftly replacing negative thoughts upon arising are imperative. This is because negative thoughts and self-criticism can be detrimental to your overall well-being.

All occurrences in your life stem from your self-perception. In order to achieve happiness, it is crucial to condition one's mindset to cultivate happiness. Subsequently, you will draw in individuals who exude joy and positivity, effectively enhancing your life, rather than relying on others to solely dictate your state of happiness.

Indicators that Your Manifestation Is Imminent

F

Faith, being the fundamental essence of optimistic aspirations, constitutes a vital constituent for the realization of desired outcomes. Lacking in faith will hinder the manifestation of your desires. At times, maintaining belief becomes challenging when confronted with circumstances that appear bereft of any semblance of hope.

Often, it is at the point when one begins to believe that overcoming a challenging circumstance is beyond their grasp, that the cosmos aligns to provide a discernible indication. One can actualize any desired outcome through unwavering belief that all circumstances will ultimately align harmoniously in one's favour. You are in closer proximity to realizing your aspirations than you perceive, consequently, exercise vigilance in identifying the indicators.

Here are five (5) indicators that your manifestation is in close proximity;

You are privy to indications and meaningful coincidences.

As you approach the realization of your desires, you will start to observe indications and coincidences. These manifestations could manifest as recurring numerical patterns, vibrant rainbows, delicate white feathers, and other symbolic representations that elicit a spiritual connection with one's guiding spirit or divine entity.

Eventually, I started observing the recurring occurrence of the numerical sequence 11:11 in various locations. It greatly perturbed me as I encountered the figures on a daily basis. I may occasionally glance at my phone and find that the time displays 11:11am or 11:11pm, or awaken inexplicably during slumber just to verify the time and behold the digits 11:11.

Certain individuals have the potential to encounter mentions of their desired manifestations through various media outlets such as radio, television, and newspapers. These indicators suggest that your manifestation is within proximity. Typically, this constitutes an individualized encounter that can only be personally observed by yourself.

Upon observing these indications and coincidences, take a moment to introspect and maintain steadfast confidence that you are actualizing your aspirations.

You feel high energy.

An unmistakable indication that you are nearing the realization of your aspirations is the emergence of a deep sense of enthusiasm toward life. You have transitioned from perceiving life as a burden to instead recognizing it as a source of blessings. Each morning upon awakening, a profound sense of anticipation arises within you, as you are keenly aware that greatness awaits and invariably manifests throughout the day. One comes to recognize that all circumstances are, in fact, aligning favorably for oneself.

Once you begin experiencing heightened enthusiasm in every aspect, it would prove detrimental to your well-being should you succumb to the belief that imminent failure awaits. There is a prevailing belief held by certain individuals that when circumstances begin to fall into place inexplicably and remarkably well, it often serves as a forewarning of imminent misfortune. By adopting such a mindset, they inadvertently undermine their own progress and consequently experience transient happiness, validating their initial anxieties.

When one begins to experience such an overwhelming surge of energy, it is important to refrain from dismissing it as an unrealistic occurrence. Rather, it is advised to embrace the present and strive to prolong the experience. So long as you consistently maintain a state of high energy, you will gradually develop a level of resilience that will lead to the automatic cessation of any self-destructive behaviors you may engage in.

The test of faith.

The examination of one's faith serves as a significant indication that the realization of their desires is imminent. Prior to the realization of your aspirations, your faith will undergo examination to ensure your precise understanding of your desires.

Consider, for instance, that you aspire to attract a caring life partner into your existence, with a specific vision of the type of companion you seek. It should not come as a surprise if you begin to encounter individuals with unpleasant dispositions and incompatible attitudes. Typically, this examination is conducted to ascertain that an individual possesses not only an absence of undesirable attributes but also a compassionate nature.

In instances where your desires do not manifest according to your intentions, view them as opportunities to demonstrate and strengthen your faith. When embarking on the manifestation of your desires, it is crucial to bear in mind that you are experiencing an elevation to a superior realm. To ascend to a higher plane, life presents you with trials to assess your worthiness before bestowing advancement upon you.

You have ceased to dwell on past events.

When one remains attached to the past, it becomes arduous to bring forth that which one yearns for. Holding onto the past suggests that your most successful moments have already occurred. The past has become a perpetual memory, with no practical necessity to dwell upon it when there are abundant prospects lying ahead.

An unmistakable indication that your manifestation is approaching is when you cease to be emotionally attached to past circumstances. You have lost interest in reflecting upon your past experiences. You possess a considerable inclination towards embracing the present moment, coupled with a strong sense of optimism regarding the future and the potential it holds for you.

The most favorable moments are awaiting you; they are yet to occur. This is the mindset of an individual in close proximity to the realization of their aspirations. With a profound sense of optimism and eager anticipation for what lies ahead, you will effortlessly materialize all that destiny has in store for you.

You create room for the influx of fresh energy.

When one's energy ascends to a heightened frequency, any elements that are incongruous with this elevated vibration will ultimately dissipate or diminish. You will start to observe a transformation in the company you keep, occupational pursuits, and undertakings, encompassing anything that depletes your vitality.

Similar energies gravitate towards each other, and only those of a corresponding nature will be drawn to you. Any individual or entity not conforming to your newly attained vibration will naturally dissipate, creating room for fresh energy to manifest.

When one begins to observe acquaintances with whom they were once closely connected gradually becoming distant, or when they no longer experience a sense of ease in the company of individuals with whom they were previously amicable, it is important not to be disheartened or perturbed. Instead, one should recognize that any relationships that do not align with their vibrational energy will naturally dissipate, making space for harmonious connections that are in resonance with their own positive frequencies.

Your Manifestation Is Close.
These indicators that your manifestation is in close proximity are typically unmistakable and highly apparent. In my personal belief, observing the numerical sequence 11:11 can be interpreted as a means by which the universe communicates with me, conveying the message that all aspects of existence are unfolding in accordance with a higher and predetermined purpose.

What are some discernible indications that you have observed in previous instances which indicate that the realization of your desired outcome is in close proximity? Do you frequently observe occurrences of identical numbers such as 11:11, 222, 444, or any other similar numerical patterns?

Addressing an Erroneous Coding Situation

You have now acquired an understanding of the process by which a subconscious program is created and its consequential impact on one's life. The subsequent inquiry pertains to discerning the empowering or constraining nature of a subconscious program. What course of action should one undertake if the unconscious programming yields unfavorable outcomes in one's life?

The indicator corresponds to the sensation experienced. As previously mentioned, when one experiences a sense of discomfort, the subconscious mind sends signals indicating the presence of an issue. It is imperative to direct one's focus towards one's feelings and emotions.

It is my belief that you possess a multitude of aspirations that you are eager to accomplish. Now, select one of your aspirations and direct your attention towards an individual who has accomplished a similar aspiration. He can be located by utilizing your preferred search engine. If one desires wealth, they may input the phrase "wealthiest individuals globally" into the search bar. Pay attention to the emotions that arise within you when you observe his presence. What is your emotional response when you gaze upon him?

Do you experience adverse emotions such as resentment, feelings of inadequacy, fear, and so on? Do you feel uncomfortable? Do you attest to his poverty? Do you hold the belief that his wealth is a result of exploiting others?

If one experiences negative emotions, it is an indicator that their subconscious programming is not providing adequate support. This task can be effectively resolved due to your prior experience with it, employing the Sedona Method.

Discover the underlying emotion associated with the situation at hand, and subsequently inquire, "Am I capable of relinquishing this particular sentiment?" Am I inclined to relinquish this sentiment? At what point in time? Continuously persist in asking this question until you attain a state of emotional liberation.

In addition, I would like to offer an additional valuable approach for coping with adverse emotions. Ho'oponopono, a concept originating from ancient Hawaii, can be understood as a practice of rectifying mistakes or restoring harmony within oneself. The crux of this theory revolves around the act of seeking forgiveness, demonstrating affection, and expressing gratitude for all the occurrences that have transpired in our lives. We convey our apologies in a concise manner through the utterance, 'I regret'. Please forgive me. I love you. Thank you".

Consider your aspirations and allow any negative sentiments to surface. While contemplating the matter at hand, kindly allow oneself to experience the associated sentiment, and subsequently reiterate the words, "I apologize." Please forgive me. I love you. Thank you."

Similar to the Sedona Method, it is not necessary to engage in contemplation or analysis; rather, one must direct their attention towards the repetition of these affirmations. Every time you recite the four sentences, you are purging adverse memories from your consciousness.

Both the Sedona Method and Ho'oponopono demonstrate considerable efficacy when it comes to facilitating the relinquishment or dissolution of negative emotions that are harbored within one's psyche and physical being. By relinquishing the negative emotion, you simultaneously release the underlying subconscious program linked to it.

Apply this approach to your other aspirations as well. Observe the individual who has successfully realized the identical aspiration. When experiencing a sense of well-being or positive emotions, it is indicative that your subconscious mind is providing you with its unwavering support. Proceed to the subsequent aspiration.

If you experience unease or negative emotional states, it is necessary to address and manage them as a priority. Otherwise, you will never attain your aspiration.

Step 3- Convey Appreciation To The Universe

To further your journey towards achieving success through harmony, it is imperative to convey your appreciation to the cosmos. Let us explore the significance of this matter and ascertain the means by which you can achieve this objective.

Importance of Being Thankful

One may inquire about the significance of expressing gratitude at this juncture. In order to facilitate comprehension, allow us to provide an illustrative example. Envisage, if you will, a scenario in which you provided assistance to another individual. Now, one would anticipate that individual to at the very least express a courteous expression of gratitude towards you. If they didn't, you'd obviously feel bad and wouldn't want to do anything nice for them again. Nevertheless, in the event that they express their gratitude for your assistance and exhibit politeness towards you, you would naturally feel inclined to display even greater kindness and amicability towards them.

In like manner, as you express profound gratitude to the cosmos for bestowing upon you diverse blessings and treasures, your affirmative thoughts imbued with gratefulness radiate outward into the expanse of the universe. The cosmic realm acknowledges your communication, accepts your expressions of appreciation, and proceeds to bestow further benevolence upon you. It initiates the delivery of increasingly remarkable and extraordinary entities that facilitate the manifestation of every single one of your numerous aspirations. In order to avail oneself of the advantages provided by the law of attraction, it is essential to commence the process of identifying and acknowledging one's blessings, followed by expressing gratitude for them.

Developing Awareness of Your Fortunate Circumstances

Attaining a profound state of consciousness and cultivating an enlightened appreciation for the abundant blessings bestowed upon you are crucial endeavors for attaining tranquility, a profound sense of contentment, and effectively manifesting desired outcomes through the practice of relaxation. Achieving genuine satisfaction and achieving a state of inner tranquility necessitate your willingness to acknowledge and fully appreciate the myriad small and significant joys bestowed upon you in life. Hence, to attain genuine happiness and attract all things positive into your life, it is crucial to direct your attention towards cultivating mindfulness of your blessings.

"Presented herein is a splendid practice capable of aiding in the identification and appreciation of one's blessings:

- Retrieve your personal diary and inscribe 'I express gratitude for' at the header of a new sheet.

- Furthermore, it is imperative to duly deliberate on five distinct elements in your life that have unequivocally contributed to the facilitation, enhancement, or amelioration of your overall lifestyle. As an example, one can consider the blessings bestowed upon them such as adequate housing, nourishing sustenance, electrical power, the presence of their child, and the possession of an automobile, to mention just a few.

- Subsequently, it is necessary to compose a brief annotation accompanying each benediction, delving into the advantageous effects it brings and the transformative impact it would have on one's life if deprived of such a blessing. For example, my quality of life has been considerably enhanced due to the presence of my car, which affords me the flexibility to conveniently commute to any desired destination. It has significantly enhanced the convenience of my daily transportation arrangements, and if it were not for this, the ease of my travel would be significantly reduced. "It facilitates the conservation of both time and energy, for which I am profoundly thankful. I express my deep gratitude for this extraordinary boon that has bestowed upon my life." Additionally, compose a note expressing appreciation and gratitude corresponding to each bestowed blessing.

Upon completion of this exercise, a profound sense of satisfaction will envelop you, accompanied by a newfound realization of the multitude of blessings in your life.

It is necessary for you to daily recognize and articulate your happiness pertaining to five newly discovered blessings.

Consistently engaging in this straightforward strategy will begin to foster a sense of indebtedness to the universe. One will gradually come to realize that joy resides in the small joys of existence and in acknowledging one's blessings, even if it pertains to something as basic as having access to clean drinking water, for there exists a multitude of individuals across the globe who lack such a privilege. This will assist you in mitigating your unfavorable and anxiety-inducing emotions that contribute to a lack of gratitude. As one begins to develop gratitude for their existence, they gradually acquire a sense of tranquility within themselves. This tranquility facilitates the actualization of your objectives.

Being Optimistic

Optimistic individuals are those who make a conscious decision to anticipate positive outcomes in life, whereas pessimistic individuals have a inclination to anticipate that circumstances will consistently turn unfavorable. To put it differently, optimists focus their attention on the donut, while pessimists fixate on the absence of something within it. Ultimately, it boils down to their underlying mindset. It is ingrained in human nature to have an inherent anticipation of negative events and a propensity to steer clear of them. This is primarily because during the era of hunting and gathering, individuals who exhibited a more cautious approach were at a reduced risk of falling victim to predatory animals. Nonetheless, it must be acknowledged that the present time does not expose us to such treacherous conditions, and engaging in a relentless pursuit of the unfavorable aspects of situations merely augments one's anguish and impedes the willingness to undertake novel ventures.

If one aspires to achieve a particular objective, it is highly advantageous to set ambitious goals. Limiting one's thinking can hinder the ability to evaluate potential opportunities, particularly given the current era where entrepreneurs endeavor to surpass each other by delivering exemplary services. There exist numerous factors that can contribute to unfavorable outcomes, however, it is important to acknowledge the potential for circumstances to indeed align in your favor. The ultimate decision lies in your hands to determine which perspective you prioritize. Do not allow oneself to be excessively preoccupied with weighing the advantages and disadvantages, scrutinizing historical data regarding past failures, or attempting to establish pragmatic projections. Instead, embrace a mindset that fosters originality and visionary thinking. Ensure that you are fully prepared to exert the necessary effort in transforming your ideas into tangible outcomes.

In numerous investigations pertaining to self-made millionaires, it is a prevailing pattern to observe that a substantial proportion of them possessed a premonition of their triumph. They typically exhibit a propensity towards optimism and enthusiasm. Several individuals who are among the wealthiest in contemporary society accumulated their fortunes by implementing concepts that initially appeared ludicrous, but ultimately resulted in significant triumph. They exhibit a highly receptive manner towards ideas, consistently seeking avenues for practical implementation and engaging in continuous brainstorming to resolve problems. Indeed, it is not infrequent to discover that during their early stages, they encountered a greater number of individuals who expressed skepticism regarding the feasibility of their aspirations. However, they exhibited the audacity to commence nonetheless and the fortitude to persist in the face of adversity, ultimately leading them to their current accomplishments.

Advantages of a Positive Outlook

Individuals with an optimistic outlook experience lower levels of loneliness compared to pessimistic individuals, owing to their enthusiastic disposition. Individuals with an optimistic disposition typically exhibit a fervent response towards individuals and circumstances, perpetually seeking opportunities to transform challenges into pathways to success. This appealing attribute significantly draws others towards optimists, thereby resulting in an increased connectivity with people. However, in contrast, individuals with a pessimistic outlook tend to repel others, resulting in their own social alienation. This phenomenon can be attributed to the perception held by a considerable number of individuals, wherein pessimistic individuals are regarded as harboring detrimental mindsets, leading others to naturally distance themselves from such individuals. Pessimistic individuals possess the ability to identify issues in nearly every circumstance, frequently engaging in complaining and expressing dissatisfaction. Consequently, their negative perspectives consistently have a detrimental impact on the mood and outlook of those around them.

Individuals with an optimistic outlook tend to experience a greater number of accomplishments and triumphs in various aspects of their lives. This phenomenon can be attributed to their optimistic outlook on the future, as well as the subconscious mind's tendency to manifest our predominant thoughts, resulting in the realization of their success. It could also be attributable to their anticipation of achieving success, thereby intensifying their drive to diligently pursue their objectives in order to manifest their anticipated outcomes. A person with a pessimistic outlook tends to identify potential challenges in any objective, thus diminishing their motivation to exert significant effort as they anticipate inevitable failure. Individuals with an optimistic outlook on life have been observed to receive a greater number of employment opportunities and advancements. This apparent correlation may be attributed to their affability in comparison to pessimistic individuals, as well as their genuine anticipation of securing such positions and advancements.

Positive thinkers exhibit greater fortitude in confronting challenges. This attribute holds immense significance in both personal and professional domains, as challenges and obstacles inherently exist within the fabric of human existence. The result of any given circumstance is invariably influenced by an individual's reaction to an adverse occurrence. A pessimist will acquiesce to the predicament, engaging in constant pondering and rationalizing their beliefs regarding potential failures. However, individuals with an optimistic outlook seek to identify the underlying message within the circumstance and subsequently endeavor to devise strategies for resolving the issue or leveraging it to their benefit. They substantiate the aphorism which posits that success is not determined by the number of times one stumbles, but by the number of times one regains composure, perseveres, and attempts once more.

Optimism fosters self-confidence. When an individual maintains an optimistic outlook, they harbor a sense of hopefulness regarding the prospective brightness of their forthcoming days. If you possess a business concept that you aspire to implement and which you hold a positive outlook on, your belief in your abilities will be reinforced. When individuals surmount obstacles without succumbing to them, their self-assurance will be enhanced. Conversely, individuals with a pessimistic outlook often lack self-assurance in their own abilities and aspirations, as they maintain a perpetual anticipation of unfavorable outcomes while remaining in perpetual anticipation for the manifestation of undesirable circumstances. Experiencing a lack of assurance in one's future becomes challenging when there is an anticipation of failure, leading pessimistic individuals to harbor fearful and apprehensive thoughts.

Positive thinking nurtures imagination and inventive thinking. Individuals who possess a positive outlook on life often harbor ambitious aspirations, which they maintain hope will ultimately materialize. This prompts them to conceive novel and innovative methods to realize their aspirations. This innovation is additionally advantageous in addressing issues since it typically demonstrates resilient in the face of challenges, steadfastly refusing to be overcome by them. Conversely, individuals with a pessimistic outlook often exhibit a limited perspective on existence. They invest a considerable amount of time in anticipating the potential consequences and dedicating even more time to contemplating problems as they occur, thereby seldom granting themselves the opportunity to perceive those problems as potential sources of inspiration.

Individuals with an optimistic outlook demonstrate heightened ability in effectively managing stress and have a tendency to maintain better overall wellbeing. This is due to their perspective of perceiving challenges as prospects, and their ability to remain less affected by situations compared to individuals with a pessimistic outlook. In terms of one's well-being, it has been observed that individuals derive greater health benefits owing to their inherent tendency to maintain a mindset that discourages illness. Optimists anticipate a swifter recuperation during illness and appear to exhibit greater tolerance for pain in comparison to individuals with a pessimistic outlook. This is the reason why medical professionals tend to abstain from conducting surgeries on individuals with depression, as these individuals often harbor pessimistic expectations. Additionally, it has been observed that individuals who maintain a positive outlook on life generally exhibit reduced levels of blood pressure. This phenomenon can be attributed to the fact that stress causes an elevation in blood pressure, while individuals who possess an optimistic outlook tend to demonstrate superior stress management skills, thereby exhibiting more effective responses to stressful circumstances.

Optimistic individuals tend to engage in more carefully evaluated risks compared to their pessimistic counterparts. When presented with an idea, optimists diligently seek avenues to effectively bring these concepts into tangible fruition. This implies that they frequently exhibit a greater receptiveness towards novel, occasionally perilous approaches and concepts that they perceive as enhancing their likelihood of achievement. In contrast, individuals with a pessimistic outlook tend to foresee failure in advance and frequently opt for cautious approaches. Generally, pessimists have been noted to engage in bad risks such as experimenting with drugs and bad behaviors for the immediate thrill that they provide. This could possibly be attributed to the fact that pessimism does not typically result in the generation of the hormones associated with positive emotions, such as endorphins, serotonin, and dopamine, which are released during optimistic thinking or when envisioning favorable outcomes. However, these risks do contribute to the release of said hormones.

Individuals with an inclination towards optimism generally tend to assume greater accountability for their own lives. They implement more extensive strategies to enhance their situation. They experience significantly greater levels of happiness and demonstrate a superior ability to effectively manage stress. This is because individuals typically have a forward-looking orientation and seldom engage in retrospective thinking unless they are reflecting upon the insights gained from past experiences. Pessimistic individuals commonly evaluate their lives through the lens of their past experiences and the perception that things unfavorably never seem to come to fruition. This mode of living often engenders a sense of helplessness in their ability to alter their circumstances, consequently fostering undesirable dispositions. In this context, individuals with a pessimistic outlook exhibit a tendency to assume the role of passive recipients in their life circumstances, whereas optimists typically adopt a proactive stance in managing their lives.

Strategies for Cultivating a Positive Outlook

One may consider initiating the process by adopting an optimistic outlook.

Optimism is a mindset that can be consciously adopted, reflecting an individual's deliberate decision. In the same manner that one has the option to perceive the potential pitfalls of a situation, one also has the capacity to direct their focus towards envisioning the potential for success in that very same situation. You have the option to perceive every challenge as an impediment or to regard each circumstance as an opportunity for personal growth. As eloquently expressed by Winston Churchill, "The individual inclined towards pessimism is prone to perceiving a challenge in every instance of opportunity." The individual driven by optimism perceives potential within every challenge. The decision to foster optimism lies solely within your control.

One can cultivate a more optimistic outlook by intentionally surrounding oneself with individuals who embody optimism, while purposefully distancing oneself from individuals who exhibit pessimistic tendencies. One's character is influenced by the companions they choose, and by consciously selecting individuals of a certain caliber to surround oneself with, one will experience a transference of their fervor into their own life. Occasionally, individuals who hold pessimistic viewpoints may include your immediate family members or colleagues, and it may prove challenging to entirely avoid their presence. Under the circumstances, it would be prudent for you to commence minimizing the amount of time you allocate to their company, and refrain from articulating your thoughts to them in order to safeguard your positive outlook on these ideas.

You have the opportunity to acquire stress management techniques that serve as reminders to distance yourself from negative thoughts (pessimism). Meditation, the practice of yoga, and the utilization of deep breathing techniques constitute effective means to cultivate a sense of tranquility in the mind. They mitigate stress in your body by effectively lowering your blood pressure and inducing a state of tranquility in your cognitive faculties. When you have achieved a state of tranquility, you enhance your capacity to devise solutions and contemplate measured responses to various situations. An equally efficacious technique involves the utilization of positive affirmations to serve as a constant reminder to remain composed. Illustrative instances consist of phrases such as 'I am capable of accomplishing this,' 'This challenging situation will eventually be resolved,' and 'I maintain a perpetually tranquil state.' These affirmations should be recurrently recited, either vocally or internally, while facing oneself in the mirror, until a state of calmness is achieved.

One additional approach to maintaining a positive outlook is to be mindful of the type of information you expose yourself to. For a heightened sense of optimism, it would be advisable to engage with motivational literature, articles, and messages. One may avail themselves of the opportunity to view optimistic videos through various online platforms, such as YouTube. Similarly, one may choose to engage in the consumption of audio recordings, such as tapes or podcasts, featuring individuals who possess a positive outlook or indulge in the listening of lively musical compositions. It is equally recommended that you exercise discretion in managing exposure to unfavorable information by limiting frequent engagement with the news or printed media. This is due to the fact that a significant portion of current news is strategically oriented towards increasing viewership by focusing on negative content. If you are engaged in a profession that demands you to stay abreast of current events, it is advisable to abstain from perusing news during the early hours of the morning or late in the evening, as they can significantly influence the way you commence your day and the quality of your sleep, respectively.

Engaging in physical activity presents an additional uncomplicated method to foster a more optimistic outlook. Engaging in physical exercise stimulates the production of endorphins in the brain, which effectively enhance mood, instilling a sense of happiness and greater enthusiasm. Engaging in regular physical activity will contribute to a sense of emotional well-being, in addition to the considerable health benefits it offers. Engaging in physical activity often engenders a sense of self-satisfaction and body appreciation, prompting individuals to exert greater effort in their endeavors with the aim of forging a more promising trajectory for their own future. By combining this with the practice of selecting nutritious food, improving sleep patterns, and increasing hydration, individuals are likely to experience heightened levels of energy and enhanced motivation to actively pursue their aspirations.

It is advisable to exercise caution and balance your optimism with tangible actions. Engaging in positive thoughts without subsequent concrete actions is essentially indulging in wishful thinking, thus leading to no tangible progress. It is imperative to balance your optimism with integrity by seeking optimal outcomes while considering the prevailing facts and circumstances. One's reliability and esteem grow when they possess the ability to accurately articulate the existing truths, even as they endeavor in the pursuit of improvement. This holds particular significance in the realm of business, as it is imperative to avoid appearing excessively self-assured and committing to deliverables beyond your capabilities.

Positive outlook is a cognitive stance distinguished by the capacity to envisage a prospective replete with opportunities and strive towards the realization of that vision. If you possess aspirations that you aim to actively pursue, it is vital that you possess unwavering conviction in your ability to effectively realize them. This is due to our existence in an expansive cosmic realm where nearly any outcome is feasible, and adopting a pessimistic attitude proves futile. The majority of the wealthiest individuals in the world exhibit the trait of optimism. It is an exceedingly captivating attribute that appeals to both customers and investors while safeguarding against despondency in the face of challenges. Please bear in mind that adopting a pessimistic outlook may be facile, while it is the embracing of optimism that truly enables one to overcome challenges.

During instances of adversity, do you tend to dwell upon the occurrence of unfavorable events, or do you strive to proactively identify measures that can be taken to ameliorate the situation? The initial response epitomizes an unequivocal indication of pessimism, whereas the subsequent reaction serves as a testament to optimism. Does the negative mindset offer any potential benefit or improvement to the situation?

To achieve success, it is essential to be prepared to address and navigate through the criticisms of those who harbor ill will towards you, as encountering such individuals is inevitable. You are required to cultivate the disposition, mindset, and resilience to effectively manage feedback, encompassing both favorable and unfavorable remarks, with particular emphasis on the latter. Triumphs engender attention, and subsequently draw individuals who harbor animosity towards you for a plethora of motives, a majority of which shall remain opaque and inscrutable. Every accomplished individual, including yourself, shall encounter critique and scrutiny.

Achievement attracts both proponents and detractors. Those who harbor ill will towards you will express their discontent due to feelings of envy or jealousy, hence, it would be advisable not to be taken aback by such behavior.

Ensure that you possess sufficient readiness to receive constructive feedback and demonstrate fortitude in overcoming such critiques, thereby achieving amplified levels of prosperity. Utilizing criticism as a catalyst for further achievements is the most effective approach. Across various platforms, most notably on social media, individuals who have achieved success often face a relentless barrage of unmerited and vitriolic criticism.

Now that you are embarking on a path towards greater achievements, it is imperative that you acquaint yourself with the concept of criticism and equip yourself to effectively handle it. Despite its harshness, criticism can serve as a valuable tool that you can leverage to enhance your personal development and achieve overall success. Numerous motivational coaches and speakers espouse the idea that in order to attain significant success, individuals must possess the willingness to endure dislike or even disdain. Initially, it is imperative to attain a comprehensive perception of the individuals with whom you will be engaging, namely, those who harbor negative sentiments.

These individuals primarily exhibit feelings of anger and openly express their accumulated frustrations, which ultimately reflects their underlying emotional vulnerability and fragility. In essence, these individuals harbor animosity towards you due to your accomplishments that elude their grasp.

The inquiry that demands your consideration in order to assess your capacity to endure possible criticism centers around your willingness to accept critique while striving towards achieving your desires. If one aims to avoid the criticism of those who harbor animosity, the most assured approach is to abstain from taking any action, as you are well aware of the consequences that such inaction will ultimately yield. The sole individual who is impervious to criticism is the individual who refrains from taking any action. Adverse feedback from detractors is an inevitable repercussion of accomplishments, therefore, it is imperative to remain impervious to the dissonance of negative voices. The fact that you are drawing the attention and scrutiny of others suggests that you are onto something truly remarkable.

It is important to bear in mind that not all individuals may partake in your elation, and it is imperative to acknowledge this reality when fostering a mindset oriented towards monetary prosperity and accomplishment. The paramount aspect in handling criticism lies within your approach towards it. It is imperative to harness the adverse energy as a catalyst to propel oneself towards greater accomplishments or improvements. Do not allow criticism and animosity to diminish your self-assurance and divert you from your aspirations. Undoubtedly, by treating the hater's criticism in the same manner as any other feedback you have previously received, you will triumph over it.

Consider this - how do you utilize the remaining feedback you receive? It is employed to assess one's current position in order to facilitate necessary adaptations towards the intended destination. Adopt a similar approach when faced with negative criticism. Indeed, valuable feedback can be found within the critical remarks provided by the detractors.

Below Are Several Advantages Of Practicing Fasting

DFasting facilitates the growth of one's faith. Upon careful observation, I have noticed that fasting invariably leads to positive outcomes, prompting me to develop an inclination towards engaging in fasting for various reasons. There exist varying degrees of faith, and when one continually observes benevolent occurrences orchestrated by a higher power after extended periods of anticipation, specifically when situations seemed precarious and capable of causing significant damage, yet divine intervention came into play subsequent to periods of fasting and prayer, it instills an elevated level of faith to place greater reliance on God for future guidance.

E) Fasting can effectively assist individuals in regulating their appetite, particularly those aiming to reduce caloric intake. Upon careful observation, it has come to my attention that engaging in dry fasting exclusively consisting of fruits subsequent to 6 pm results in a detoxification process, leading to a state of heightened physical and mental well-being characterized by a notable sense of lightness and liberation within my body. Upon the conclusion of the third day of abstaining from food, I shall observe a discernible reduction in body weight and a noticeable improvement in the vitality and complexion of the skin.

F) It facilitates the development of one's spiritual fortitude and prowess. On numerous occasions, upon commencing a period of fasting, I consistently observe a significant alteration in my dream patterns overnight. Specifically, my dream imagery becomes remarkably vivid and there is a noticeable intensification of my spiritual fortitude compared to prior states. I anticipate that my dreams will bring forth revelations of emancipation and progress. In those visions, I shall witness the manifestation of divine influence within me, performing feats that surpass my own expectations, even in the absence of fasting. This serves as a definite indication that by incorporating fasting into your prayer practice, your spiritual fortitude and efficacy will be heightened. No force will have the ability to hinder such great power, as it originates from a higher source that has fortified your inner being, as stated in the biblical passage Philippians 4:13 - "I am capable of achieving all things through the empowerment bestowed upon me."

G) You shall experience extraordinary miracles and significant breakthroughs as a result of fasting. The practice of fasting and praying has yielded remarkable outcomes in my life, as the benevolence of God has been evident during moments of my utmost necessity. Following a period of abstinence and devout supplication, I have experienced favorable outcomes concerning my conjugal, monetary, and metaphysical pursuits from him. I express enduring gratitude towards him, which strengthens my confidence in him further.

Furthermore, one of the notable benefits of fasting resides in its ability to inspire a contrite heart, as it serves as a constant reminder of the requirement for personal holiness before approaching the divine presence of God.

The inhabitants of Nineveh exhibited remorse towards their immoral actions, consequently receiving divine clemency. Regularly engaging in fasting will consistently place you in a state whereby you rid your heart from the weight of transgressions and resentments, in preparation for entering into the divine presence.

We express profound adoration for God by frequently abstaining from food, as doing so allows us to perceive the magnificence of God in our circumstances whenever we encounter Him. Consequently, we develop affection towards others due to the immense love bestowed upon us by God in response to our supplications.

J) It facilitates our understanding of our life's priorities and the appropriate approach to pursue them. When engaging in fasting, individuals are bestowed with divine guidance and instruction, which serve as a compass leading them towards the virtuous path that leads to accomplishment.

Whenever we abstain from food, we rid ourselves of the oppressive forces of injustice and liberate ourselves from the burden of malevolent influences, thereby opening the doors for divine favor and the occurrence of significant advancements in our lives. This is in accordance with the teachings of Isaiah 58:6-7.

This assists us in developing a deep yearning for God and a fervent dedication to His endeavors...Mark 4:19 states that "the concerns of this earthly life, the allure of material wealth, and the desires for other worldly things can suffocate the teachings of God, rendering them void of productivity."

When one possesses both an ardent yearning and unwavering conviction, events will swiftly and seamlessly manifest within one's personal journey.

-Esther Hicks

What is Manifesting?

Have you ever pondered upon the magnificence that would ensue if your profound aspirations were to be granted? I am referring to the aspirations characterized by a lifestyle that embraces rapid living, fervent love, and premature mortality. The aspirations that reside nearest to your core being. Desires that yield fulfillment, exhilaration, and enable a purposeful existence. Moreover, they may even evoke a sense of intimidation in you.

Money. Love. Success. Envision yourself positioned at the heart of the situation. But how?

Allow me to elucidate upon an inherent mystical ability residing within us, commonly referred to as manifestation. It is the realm where our convictions, cognitions, and emotional states exert profound sway over the manifestations that enter our existence. It exerts a profound impact on the very essence of our reality, precipitating events and outcomes.

There is an absence of mystical and spiritual ceremonies. There is no manner by which one can surreptitiously manipulate the behavior of others. It is impossible to compel individuals to engage in actions contrary to their own volition. Requisite for success is a mindset of receptiveness coupled with a substantial level of positive thinking.

Individuals have employed the practice of manifestation to attain their utmost desires in life. Relationships. Careers. Money. Happiness and peace. The possibilities are vast! However, please bear in mind that the process of manifestation does not occur instantaneously. It is imperative that you adopt a proactive approach in order to achieve your goals. However, placing faith in the systematic approach can yield profound consequences in one's life.

It is not difficult to achieve the manifestation of your desires. The crucial aspect lies in comprehending that it is indeed a collaborative endeavor involving both oneself and the vast expanse of the Universe. It is imperative that action be taken in order to make this collaboration successful.

For individuals aspiring to achieve manifesting success, the initial requirement is the cultivation of a resolute intention. This aspiration should resonate deeply within your being. It is essential to have a clear understanding of your genuine desires, rather than pursuing what you believe societal expectations dictate. It is imperative to possess an unwavering and authentic fervor to attain or construct the desired objective. The more precise and steadfast your intention is, the swifter the actualization process will unfold. Subsequently, you mentally picture yourself possessing it.

An additional crucial aspect of the process of manifestation pertains to one's conviction or faith. One must possess unshakeable faith in one's ability to accomplish their objectives, akin to the unwavering self-assurance exhibited by Kanye. The greater your conviction in your objective and its attainability, the more assured you will be in its realization. It is imperative that you relinquish any form of resistance or constricting beliefs that might impede your progress towards attaining your objectives. Occasionally, resistance manifests as adverse internal dialogue. Adopting pessimistic attitudes towards your objectives will not lead to the realization of the outcome you seek.

The final aspect to consider is the anticipation or the projected outcome. Envision yourself experiencing the fulfillment of your aspirations. Imagine that you are presently undergoing and deriving pleasure from them. It is imperative for you to anticipate that the Universe is delivering precisely what you have requested of it.

Four Fundamental Actions for Manifestation

Step 1: Request Assistance

This marks the initiation point - making selections and establishing objectives. Reflect upon the query, "What objective do I aspire to that is congruous with my innermost desires?" Subsequently, determine a specific endeavor or achievement that you wish to manifest or actualize in your existence. It is plausible that it could be a fresh employment opportunity. A dream home. A new love relationship. To effect a transformation within oneself. In order to enhance one's financial resources or achieve a sculpted physique. Please endeavor to provide the utmost clarity and specificity in expressing your intention. Let us consider a scenario where you aspire to encounter your ideal life partner. Interrogate oneself by pondering, "How would the physical appearance of this individual manifest?" or "What characteristics and virtues define the personality of this individual?" or "What mannerisms and core values resonate with this individual?" Mastery of this phase shall initiate a transformative process within the depths of one's subconscious, where the genesis of all manifestations transpires.

The effectiveness of the law of attraction is contingent upon the level of lucidity in regards to your intention. Occasionally, one may opt for an intention that is lacking in strength or experience uncertainty surrounding them. In the event of such occurrence, endeavor to thoroughly investigate the underlying causes of your uncertainties, apprehensions, or internal disagreements. It may be necessary for you to acknowledge your hesitations and address any emotional or cognitive barriers you may be experiencing. In certain instances, vacillation can serve as an indicator that the objective you have selected may not be well-suited for you. It is imperative to articulate your desires with utmost clarity and precision. If one remains uncertain about their desires, they will inevitably acquire numerous things about which they remain uncertain. One cannot attain what they lack certainty in.

Your objectives must align with your genuine aspirations, rather than being dictated by societal expectations. They ought to be the matters that occupy your thoughts consistently. Factors that one is cognizant of that will enhance the standard of their lifestyle. Your aspirations should be a true reflection of your identity and personal values.

If you are new to the practice of manifesting, it is advised to select goals that are within your perceived realm of attainability. This will enable you to optimize your sense of accomplishment. Additionally, it will help mitigate any adverse opposition or doubts surrounding your ability to achieve those goals. Once you have acquired proficiency in the art of manifesting, you can subsequently progress towards more arduous objectives.

Regardless of your objectives, issue a directive to the universe and communicate your desires to it. Words are powerful. They possess an enchanting quality with the ability to both manifest and annihilate. By issuing a directive, you will have the opportunity to manifest the desired circumstances in your life, with the possibility of a promising future ahead. You will exhibit resolute determination when confronted with challenges that seem insurmountable, while simultaneously exerting control over elements that defy regulation.

Please document your aspirations precisely as you desire. Avoid excessive analysis and refrain from limiting yourself. It is permissible to have ambitious objectives. Having a mindset that encompasses grand ideas implies being receptive to attaining substantial outcomes. Provide a comprehensive elucidation of these aspects to enhance your concentration during meditation. The more well-defined the objective, the more clearly defined the result will be.

Step 2: Visualize It

The foundational principles of visualization are uncomplicated. You construct a cognitive representation of your objective or aspiration within the confines of your thoughts, precisely as you envision it. The technique goes by the name of Creative Visualization, and further elaboration on this topic will be provided in Chapter 8. When engaging in the act of visualization, one mentally conjures an image of oneself already in possession of one's desired outcomes. Please provide an extensive account of the various details that can assist in guiding your contemplation about the emotional impact associated with the realization of those aspirations.

If you aspire to acquire the sleek and immaculate sports car. Imagine yourself having it. Consider envisioning yourself behind the wheel, appreciating its features, savoring the experience, and proudly displaying it to your companions. If such a circumstance is what you seek. Envision yourself in that scenario where every aspect unfolds according to your desires. Envision the conjecture and actions of individuals, as well as any other particulars that will engender a heightened sense of realism within you. Any method you choose to employ in order to mentally conjure scenes reflecting your objectives or aspirations can be referred to as your preferred mechanism for "visualizing."

Retain a vivid mental image of your aspiration within your cognitive faculties. Engage in the practice of affirming constructive thoughts about them. It may be articulated verbally or kept internalized. These affirmative statements serve as declarations. For example:

I am quite enamored with the stunning vista that is afforded to me from my recently-acquired beachfront vacation residence.

Or

I am in the process of developing a deep sense of self-acceptance and embracing who I truly am.

If one encounters skeptical thoughts while envisioning their goals, it is advisable not to oppose them. This will grant empowerment to those pessimistic thoughts. Allow the influx of negative thoughts to pass through your consciousness, and subsequently converge back towards your positive affirmations.

Step 3: Believe It

Regularly visualize your objective or aspiration in your thoughts. Envision your objectives during a serene contemplation, or informally throughout your day. By incorporating it into your daily routine, it will seamlessly integrate into your lifestyle and enhance your ability to project it with greater success.

The crucial aspect lies in maintaining a persistent and continuous concentration. Why? Due to the fact that the Universe reflects the thoughts that prevail in your mind. Your concentration and attentiveness are requested. By devoting your focus to the pursuit of your objectives, you evoke the principles of the Law of Attraction. It will exert a transformative influence, aligning all circumstances, individuals, and occurrences in your favor, granting your desires a newfound vitality.

Direct your attention towards your objectives with a composed demeanor, fostering a mindset of optimism and motivation. It is crucial to refrain from exerting undue pressure on your concentration. Avoid exerting excessive efforts by expending an abundance of energy in the process of visualization. This procedure ought to be a pleasurable and inherently instinctive experience for you.

As you direct your attention towards your objectives, imbue them with recurring, optimistic emotions. This is the sole amount of energy required by the Universe to transmute them, inevitably bringing about their manifestation within your realm.

Persist in your concentration until you reach your objectives. It is acceptable if you perceive a shift in your goals. Acknowledge that the previous objective is no longer beneficial, and commence pursuit of a fresh objective.

Recognize the attainment of a goal and express appreciation for it. Occasionally, we fail to acknowledge our achievements in effectively materializing our aspirations. Primarily, owing to its occurrence with utmost ease, it is essential to express gratitude to the Universe for manifesting your appeals.

Step 4: Expect It

The ultimate stage in the process of manifestation entails cultivating a sense of anticipation. Have utmost faith that the Universe is faithfully bestowing upon you your desires in a manner of utmost grace and abundance. Anticipate the manifestation of your aspirations. Visualize yourself receiving and attaining these accomplishments. It is imperative to maintain a steadfast conviction that your desires are being attained, either presently or in the immediate future. Receiving involves the cognitive, emotional, and behavioral alignment with the belief that the desired outcome has already materialized. Consider it in this manner. You already possess all the things that you desire. Take note that they will approach you, and regard them as though they are already under your ownership.

If one does not anticipate the fulfillment of their aspirations, they are impeding their manifestation in one's existence. Begin to experience a sense of gratification upon attaining your aspirations. Experiencing positive emotions such as fervor, zeal, and joy in relation to your objectives implies that you are embracing them as integral parts of your life. You are displaying a lack of opposition and positioning yourself in a manner that enables you to receive what you have requested.

Manifestation encompasses more than contemplating a concept solely on a cerebral plane. If one were to subtract the influence of emotions, there would be an insufficient amount of fuel to propel one's aspirations forward. You must feel it. It is imperative that you adopt the mentality, conduct, and language of someone who already has possession of their desires. Your thoughts determine your level of attraction. When one anticipates receiving, one shall indeed receive.

www.ingramcontent.com/pod-product-compliance
Lightning Source LLC
Chambersburg PA
CBHW050247120526
44590CB00016B/2245